GROW
AT
HOME

GROW AT HOME

A BEGINNER'S GUIDE TO FAMILY DISCIPLESHIP

Winfield Bevins

 Seedbed

Unless otherwise indicated, Scripture quotations are from The Holy Bible, English Standard Version®, ESV®, copyright © 2001 by Crossway Bibles, a division of Good News Publishers. Used by permission. All rights reserved.

Printed in the United States of America

Paperback ISBN: 978-1-62824-278-2
Mobi ISBN: 978-1-62824-279-9
ePub ISBN: 978-1-62824-280-5
uPDF ISBN: 978-1-62824-281-2

Library of Congress Control Number: 2016940300

Cover design by Strange Last Name
Page design by PerfecType, Nashville, Tennessee

SEEDBED PUBLISHING
Franklin, Tennessee
Seedbed.com

To my beautiful family:
my amazing wife, Kay,
and our three girls,
Elizabeth, Anna Belle,
and Caroline.

Contents

Foreword

My three-year-old and five-year-old show affection, competition, and malice like any siblings. When one of our kids hurts the other emotionally or physically we have a pretty typical family practice: we line them up facing each other and make the offender say the words: "I'm sorry." The victim then responds: "I forgive you."

That used to be the end of it until our kids began to add their own line to the rehearsed pattern. The part we never scripted is that at some point the original culprit began spontaneously replying back to the wounded, "I forgive you, too." For a while I thought I should correct them—the innocent one shouldn't have to be forgiven, right? But the dual "I forgive yous"—however unprompted, became a kind of family liturgy for us. Hearing my kids say it back and forth to each other, and then as they began to say it back to me after I forgave them for something, taught me about the nature of forgiveness—none of us is wholly innocent in any spat. No matter who threw the first punch, it helps all of us to hear those words regularly: "I forgive you." My kids daily teach me about God and the nature of our life with Him. I'm trying to keep up with them as I aim to teach them as well.

Our family is our first church. It's the place where we develop our first inklings of what God is like, whether someone knows they are teaching or not.

Faith is formed around the dinner table, in questions thrown back and forth from the backseat, and in bedtime conversations where the events of the previous day come rushing back and the anticipation and fears of the next day rush toward us. But when it comes to forming intentional patterns of family discipleship, many of us come up short on knowing what the building blocks are and how to incorporate them in ways that draw our children to the faith that means so much to us.

Most of us know that family discipleship is important, but we don't quite know where to begin. The truth is that there are far more resources out there about building good habits for nutrition and exercise in our kids than there are for building a strong spiritual foundation. It's simply not true that if we can get our children to church, the church will do the rest for us. We have a personal responsibility for our kids to hear the Word, learn to pray, and to know God loves them. The question that remains is just how we can do that in winsome ways that will reach their hearts.

This is why *Grow at Home* is so invaluable. Rather than a professional in Christian education, we hear words of coaching and encouragement from a fellow parent in the trenches, a dad trying daily to introduce his three daughters to the Jesus who has forever changed him.

Winfield Bevins and I became friends when we landed in the same small town in Kentucky in order to work on different aspects of shepherding seminary students into their vocation. Apart from being colleagues together, we've also been parents side by side. Anyone who spends time around someone with their family for any period of time can easily grow to know their heart, and Winfield's heart is open, generous, and wise. I'm thankful that he decided to share the fruit of what he's learned as a disciple-making parent in this little book because I know it will bless other parents trying to walk the same path. It has blessed me.

All of us who call Jesus Lord and have children who we want to grow to do the same are really discovering day by day how to disciple our families. I am a pastor and a guide for those on their way to become pastors, missionaries, or teachers of youth and children, and I see their deep desire to share Christ with others. I also see befuddlement about how it is really supposed to work between homework, sports, and music lessons, chaotic dinnertimes, and looming bedtimes.

Whether or not we came from families that provided good examples, the truth is that doing what has been done in generations before and in the same ways it has been done may not produce the same results as before, and each family has different needs and challenges. This is a personal journey, but it's not one we should try to do alone.

Grow at Home encourages and challenges parents, empowering them with tools to share the love of God in a way their children can understand. How do we teach our children to pray, to love God's Word? How do we lead them to Christ? It's good to have the words of one who cares as deeply as we do about the next generation. It's good to know that lessons taught don't have to be legalistic, idealistic, or shame-based, but that offer the full grace and love of God to and through the family.

I grew up hearing in some circles that faith is best caught, not taught; that it's our example and not our didactic teaching that provides the best foundation for faith in our homes. But what if it is really both? Jesus taught by example and action, but also by words and instruction that imparted powerful truths and demanded a response. If we wouldn't leave our children's academic development or physical health up to chance, why would do so with their spiritual health? It can be awkward and strange at first to broach these subjects if we haven't heard them addressed in a family before, but the intimacy and strength that will flow is always worth the risk of trying new things.

Those of us walking through this book together are blessed to know there are patterns, habits, disciplines, and conversations that have been practiced for centuries that will connect our first churches— our families—to the greater church that connects us all the way back to the footsteps of Christ. Growing at home is a beautiful and organic way to begin.

—Rev. Jessica LaGrone
Dean of Chapel, Asbury Theological Seminary

Introduction:
Why Family Discipleship?

"If religion is not extended to the children, what will be the outcome?"

—*John Wesley*

Why this book? Why family discipleship? There are tons of books on Christian parenting. Just take a walk through your local Christian bookstore and look around. Many of those books are immensely helpful, but few of them address the critical role that parents play in shaping children's lives through family discipleship.

So what is family discipleship? Maybe you have never heard of the term or are not sure what it means. Let me begin by saying what it is not. Family discipleship is not a program or ministry of the church. Family discipleship is when parents help their children become disciples of Jesus Christ in the home through reading the Bible, praying, worshiping, and doing missions together (see Deuteronomy 6:4–9; 11:18–21; Psalm 78:5; Ephesians 6:4). I will unpack this definition of family discipleship throughout the rest of this book.

You may be thinking, "What are his qualifications for writing this book?" Well, the truth is, I am not an expert by any stretch of the imagination. *Grow at Home* is an introduction to family discipleship, written by a guy who wasn't raised in church or in a family that practiced faith in the home. I have had to learn about it the hard way. In fact, I am still learning and I don't have it all together. I have an amazing wife and three incredible little girls who have joined me on this crazy journey of faith. This book took shape around our dinner table, in our living room, and every evening in my children's rooms. They were my guinea pigs.

In addition to being a husband and father, I was the pastor of a church that was full of young families with small children for ten years. Many of these young families were new to the faith. Some of them came from broken homes with divorced parents and needed parenting role models. One of my biggest challenges was helping them integrate their faith into the home. For these reasons, I have put into writing some of the things that we found helpful with discipling our children.

Family discipleship can be both fun and educational. I have written this book as a practical guide to family discipleship for families from all ages and backgrounds. It is for both parents and children. Each chapter begins with an introduction to the topic for parents to discuss and then concludes with a practical application of the material to share with your children, called "Grow at Home." It is not like a book that you read from start to finish, rather, you can start in any of the sections and go back and forth as you choose. To get the most out of the book, you are encouraged to use the videos that correspond to different chapters to help you implement the ideas of the book at home with your family.

I invite you to begin the journey of family discipleship by using this book as a guide to help you incorporate your faith into the daily routines of your home. Join the movement that is happening in homes across North America as parents are rediscovering family discipleship. It starts in our marriages, by loving our spouses with the love of Christ. It happens by teaching, loving, and sharing our faith with our children. When we bring the gospel back into the home, it will spread through our neighborhoods and into the communities where we live. If every family in every church got serious about making disciples in the home, it would change our world. Let the journey begin!

GROW AT HOME

Chapter 1

A Parent's Responsibility

"Consider family religion not merely as a duty imposed by authority, but as your greatest privilege granted by divine grace."
—Dr. Martyn-Lloyd Jones

It doesn't take a rocket scientist to realize that traditional family life has changed over the last decade in North America. All you have to do is look around your city, neighborhood, or school, or simply turn on the television to see how family life has changed. *Leave It to Beaver* has been replaced with television shows like *Modern Family*, which promotes alternative views of family life. Statistics show that divorce rates and teen violence have been skyrocketing for the past decade in North America and England.[1]

There are obvious cultural influences that have had a significant effect on families, such as technology, television, and media. However, we can't blame it all on the culture. Christians are responsible for much of the problem as well. One of the primary reasons is that we have taken an individualistic approach to faith and this has not emphasized the corporate nature of Christianity. The result is that we have produced a generation of consumeristic, and not radically committed, disciples of Jesus Christ.

Consumeristic Christianity sees the church as a place that is all about me, my wants, and my needs; a place of goods and services, instead of being a place where we are challenged to grow, serve, give, and go back into the world in mission. The result of embracing individualism and cultural consumerism has negatively affected contemporary Christianity. Author Alan Hirsch wrote, "We can't make disciples based on a consumerist approach to the faith. We plainly cannot consume our way into discipleship . . . consumption is detrimental to discipleship."[2] For people to grow as disciples they need more than a consumeristic faith; they need a faith that is lived together.

The culture and our consumeristic Christianity have had a devastating effect on the faith of our youth. Recent statistics show that more youth are turning away from the faith than ever before: it is estimated that as many as 70–80 percent of teens who profess Christianity walk away from their faith by the end of their freshman year of college. We have to radically rethink how we are raising our children in the faith.

Several years ago Hillary Clinton famously quoted the African proverb, "It takes a village to raise a child." While there is truth in this, nothing can replace the crucial role of the family. It takes a family to raise a child. More than ever, we need to step back and rethink the importance and value of doing faith together as a family.

The answer is that we need to bring faith back into the home through family discipleship. What good is it if you make disciples of your neighbors and coworkers, yet neglect to disciple your own children? Parents, we need family discipleship. In the next few pages, I want to share some words of encouragement with parents as you seek to live out this great task of family discipleship.

A Parent's Responsibility

Parenting is an amazing responsibility. I will never forget February 25, 2004. It was the day our first daughter, Elizabeth Susanna, was born. It was the day that I became a parent. It was a very emotional day. After a long day of labor, my wife had to have a c-section. In the end, we had a beautiful, nine-pound baby girl!

Shortly after she was born, I found myself alone in a dimly lit hospital room holding Elizabeth. She was crying and I was crying too, probably for different reasons. As tears rolled down my face, I was overwhelmed with the emotion of being a new father and holding my tiny baby girl for the first time ever. I can still remember being overcome with a sense of holy responsibility. I was holding a little human that God had created and entrusted to my wife and me for safekeeping.

As I write this, Elizabeth will be ten years old in a few days. Reflecting back on that night, my sense of godly responsibility for her is still the same today as it was the day she was first born. The only difference is that she is a lot older now and I can barely pick her up!

Having children is one of life's most wonderful privileges that carries with it an amazing responsibility to shape the hearts and lives of our children. In fact, I can't think of any greater responsibility than being entrusted with a human life. We have been made stewards of the physical, emotional, and spiritual well-being of our children.

The call to "make disciples" begins in our homes first. It is our spiritual responsibility as parents to teach our children about the faith. Proverbs instructs, "Train up a child in the way he should go; even when he is old he will not depart from it" (22:6). As Christian parents, we should desire for our children to have a firm foundation and grow up to love Jesus and know what the Bible says about their lives.

Many parents believe that it is the church's responsibility to raise their children in the faith. Too often, people think that the church is more like a babysitting service to watch our kids for a few hours a week. Nothing could be further from the truth. While church is important, the Bible tells us that the home is the primary place of learning the Bible and giving moral instruction. The church is meant to support parents in discipling their children. In Deuteronomy 6:5–9, we read:

> You shall love the Lord your God with all your heart and with all your soul and with

all your might. And these words that I command you today shall be on your heart. You shall teach them diligently to your children, and shall talk of them when you sit in your house, and when you walk by the way, and when you lie down, and when you rise. You shall bind them as a sign on your hand, and they shall be as frontlets between your eyes. You shall write them on the doorposts of your house and on your gates.

This passage offers us a paradigm for raising our children in the faith and being missional families. First, it is important for parents to understand that discipleship begins with us and in us. The "words that I command you today shall be on your heart" is a message for parents. Family discipleship is not something we do for the kids, but it is for parents as well. In family discipleship, parents and children alike are shaped into disciples of Jesus Christ. I would like to encourage you to let your hearts be transformed by the same truths as your children.

Second, we are reminded that faith is not just something that we do once a week, but something that should be incorporated into the daily routines of the home. We should "teach them diligently . . .

talk of them when you sit in your house." This means we should have a regular time to teach our faith to our children. In life, we schedule what is most important to us. If you don't plan a time to talk to your children about their faith, it will most likely not happen.

We should find moments to talk about our faith throughout the day with our families. How do we spend our time? Watching television, playing video games, or shopping? Sadly, many families devote more time to these things than they do teaching their children about God, or just simply spending quality time together. There are teachable moments to share our faith with our children throughout each day. The problem is that we are too busy to take advantage of them. Choose a time that works best for you—dinner, bedtime, breakfast.

Third, faith is not meant to be confined to the home, but lived in our daily lives and in our communities. We learn as we go through life. Home is where faith learning begins, but the real world is where it is lived. Take time to stop and teach your children faith lessons in the car or at the grocery store. Christianity isn't just about knowing God, but living for Him. Children want a real faith that they connect to and live out. Make opportunities to serve in the local community and to share your faith together as a family.

Grace and Parenting

Real family discipleship is always grace-centered. There is an important connection between grace and parenting because what we believe about God's love has a direct effect on how we parent our children. In many ways, our parenting is the fruit of our theology. What we believe about God, His love, His discipline, and His forgiveness will affect how we love, forgive, and discipline our children. If we see God as a dictator, we will become a dictator to our children. If we see God as a loving, gracious, heavenly Father who has given His Son for us, then we can be loving, gracious parents who are willing to sacrificially love our children.

Children and parents both need to be reminded of God's grace. Children are never too young and parents are never too old to learn the simple truths of the gospel of Jesus Christ. We all need it! The hearts and minds of both parents and children are transformed as we grow together in our faith through the great truths of the gospel of grace.

Perhaps more that anything, the gospel of grace reminds us of our own personal need for

God's grace in our lives, our hearts, and our homes. God's grace is the foundation of Christian parenting because it begins and ends with His love for us and for our children. Grace means that our relationship with God is free and not based upon good deeds or anything that we can do. It means we can never be good enough to earn God's love. We can do nothing to make God love us more than He already does.

Grace is good news for parents because we are not perfect and we sin every single day. Christian parenting is not about our perfection, but it is about His grace and His forgiveness. When we sin and fall short, God's grace is sufficient to keep us from falling. Paul reminds us, "My grace is sufficient for you, for my power is made perfect in weakness" (2 Cor. 12:9). As a father, there have been many days when I have felt like a failure and I just wanted to give up. There have been times when I have lost my temper or said something to my family that was not out of love and I have had to repent and ask for God's forgiveness and for my family's forgiveness as well. In moments like these, we need to be reminded that God's grace is sufficient for our lives and our homes. Grace is good news for imperfect parents!

Don't Go It Alone

Parenting can be a lonely business. Sometimes we can feel like we are all alone and like nobody knows what we are going through. It is easy to sink into condemnation and compare ourselves to the parents down the street who look like they have it all together. The truth is, they probably don't. Once you begin to talk with other parents you will realize that you are not alone and that most parents feel the same way you do.

All parents face similar problems and issues, such as trying to teach our children discipline, respect, and self-control. It is a good idea to fellowship with other parents, and to feel supported in your role as a parent. See if your church offers a parenting group. If not, you can help start one. Invite unchurched parents from your neighborhood to see what a Christian family looks like. We learn together and from one another, so reach out and find a community of parents who are wrestling with the same issues that you are.

As parents, we also need mentors in our lives. Like Bilbo Baggins from *The Hobbit*, everyone needs a Gandalf, and every parent needs a mentor in their life. Our churches are full of seasoned parents who have faithfully raised their children. These men and women would love to share their parenting experiences with young parents who are just beginning their family journey. The key is being humble and willing to learn from an experienced couple who have already raised their children.

You'd be surprised how many older parents would love to mentor a young family. After we had our first child, my wife and I began to seek wisdom from older couples in our church. As a result, I can think of many men and women who have taken the time to disciple my wife and me in the art of parenting. Not to mention that these older parents are usually the best babysitters!

Be Yourself

Lastly, parents, be yourself. Don't try to be something or someone that you are not. Some people think that they need to act, dress, or talk a certain way in order to be a good parent. This is a false perception that leads many parents down the wrong road. Nobody likes it when a person is trying to be somebody or something that they are not, especially God.

I'm reminded of the movie *Fun with Dick and Jane*, starring Jim Carrey and Tea Leoni as Dick and Jane Harper, an upper-middle-class couple who resort to robbery after the company for which Dick works goes bankrupt. It's a funny parody of the downside of what can happen when we try to keep up with the Joneses. Don't end up like Dick and Jane Harper; just be yourself and God will help you take care of the rest!

The Lord wants to use your unique gifts, talents, and personality to disciple your children. No two people are the same; therefore, no two parents are the same. There is a unique home that God has created just for you. Only when we are who God has created us to be can we truly disciple our children. So be yourself, relax, and enjoy the journey of family discipleship.

Grow at Home

The Bible is at the very heart of family discipleship. It deserves a proper place in the home, not only on our bookshelves, but in our hearts and minds. Knowing what the Scriptures teach us about the family, children, and our responsibility as parents is absolutely essential to shepherding our children. Without the Bible, parenting can just become a mere form of behavior modification or psychological control. As we begin this book, I would like to encourage you to take some time to prayerfully study the following Scriptures on the family. Let them sink into your heart and inspire your faith as you take up the great task of discipling your children.

Deuteronomy 6:7: You shall teach them diligently to your children, and shall talk of them when you sit in your house, and when you walk by the way, and when you lie down, and when you rise.

Proverbs 22:6: Train up a child in the way he should go; even when he is old he will not depart from it.

Ephesians 6:4: Fathers, do not provoke your children to anger, but bring them up in the discipline and instruction of the Lord.

Proverbs 29:15: The rod and reproof give wisdom, but a child left to himself brings shame to his mother.

Colossians 3:21: Fathers, do not provoke your children, lest they become discouraged.

Proverbs 29:17: Discipline your son, and he will give you rest; he will give delight to your heart.

Proverbs 22:15: Folly is bound up in the heart of a child, but the rod of discipline drives it far from him.

Psalm 127:3–5: Behold, children are a heritage from the LORD, the fruit of the womb a reward. Like arrows in the hand of a warrior are the children of one's youth. Blessed is the man who fills his quiver with them! He shall not be put to shame when he speaks with his enemies in the gate.

2 Timothy 3:16: All Scripture is breathed out by God and profitable for teaching, for reproof, for correction, and for training in righteousness.

Proverbs 15:5: A fool despises his father's instruction, but whoever heeds reproof is prudent.

Matthew 19:14: But Jesus said, "Let the little children come to me and do not hinder them, for to such belongs the kingdom of heaven."

Proverbs 19:18: Discipline your son, for there is hope; do not set your heart on putting him to death.

1 Samuel 1:27–28: "For this child I prayed, and the LORD has granted me my petition that I made to him. Therefore I have lent him to the LORD. As long as he lives, he is lent to the LORD." And he worshiped the LORD there.

1 Samuel 2:26: Now the boy Samuel continued to grow both in stature and in favor with the LORD and also with man.

Proverbs 31:27–28: She looks well to the ways of her household and does not eat the bread of idleness. Her children rise up and call her blessed; her husband also, and he praises her.

Luke 2:52: And Jesus increased in wisdom and in stature and in favor with God and man.

Chapter 2

Rediscovering Family Worship

"They that pray in the family do well; they that pray and read the Scriptures do better; but they that pray, and read, and sing do best of all."
—*Matthew Henry*

Nothing comes more natural to a child than singing songs. Trust me, I know. I have little girls that sing everywhere they go—in the car, at home, at school, in the shower, etc. The reason children love music and singing is because God has created each one of us, young and old, to worship Him. The Bible reminds us that children are not too young to worship or understand their faith. The

Bible says, "Out of the mouth of infants and nursing babies you have prepared praise" (Matt. 21:16).

Since the birth of Christianity, prayer and worship have been essential elements of practicing our faith. Worship is the act of giving all of ourselves back to God by giving Him respect, reverence, honor, and glory. The English word means "worthship" and carries the idea of worthiness. God is worthy of our highest praise and worship. God has called us to live "to the praise of his glory" (Eph. 1:12). We are here to glorify and know the God who created us. True worship of God begins in our hearts as we give adoration, glory, and praise to God and then it manifests outwardly as we lift up our voices to God in prayer, praise, and song.

Worship is more than singing or clapping our hands; worship involves all that we are and it influences how we live our lives for God. The writer of Psalms tells us to "Worship the LORD in the splendor of holiness" (96:9). Living our lives for God in love and holiness is perhaps one of the highest forms of worship that we can offer to God (see Romans 12:10).

Rediscovering Family Worship

Worship is not just something we do on Sunday mornings, but something that should take place in our homes. Christian families everywhere are beginning to rediscover the great blessing of family worship. What is family worship? Family worship is simply coming together as a family and worshiping God in the home. In the same way we come together for a time of corporate worship in the church, we also come together in the home for a time of family worship that involves prayer, reading Scripture, and singing songs. Author Jason Helopoulos reminds us, "We need to hear about the need for family worship in our homes. . . . My hope is that our Christian homes will once again be filled with fathers, mothers, husbands, wives, children, sisters, and brothers that are worshiping to the glory of God."[1]

The truth is, your home is like a little church. The Reformers, including Martin Luther and John Calvin, promoted family worship in the home and called upon parents to disciple their children. Later, Christians in England and America carried on the emphasis on family worship and discipleship. John Wesley wrote a *Collection of Prayers for Families*, which were to be used for morning and evening prayers throughout the week. The pastoral theologian Jonathan Edwards reminds us that "Every Christian family ought to be as it were a little church."[2] In other words, parents have a moral and spiritual responsibility to make the home a place of Christian worship and discipleship. We bring the components of a worship service—which include reading the Bible, praying, and singing—into our homes through family worship.

Keep It Simple

At this point you may be thinking, "This isn't for me." or "Okay, this sounds pretty hard to do." I admit that the idea of family worship may seem a little intimidating at first, but don't let it be. Honestly, every Christian parent can lead their home in family worship. It's really not that hard. Teaching your kids about your faith and sharing in a time of family worship isn't just for trained theologians or pastors with kids. It's for all of us, including single parents, working parents, and parents who are new to the faith. Trust me, if my wife and I can do it, you can do it too.

I remember the first time we gathered together as a family to read the Bible, pray, and sing songs to the Lord. Our girls were still very young, but we made it a special time for the entire family by allowing our children to be involved in the prayers, the singing, and reading the Bible. As the parents, we provide the guidance, but everyone can play a part in your time of family worship. We let our girls share in leading the prayers and reading the Scriptures. The fact is, family worship doesn't have to be stuffy or boring, but can be fun and uplifting. Let everyone play a part and get involved in your time together.

The key to family worship is to start small and finish big. It's worth it because your children really do want to know about God. The truth is family worship is not that hard, so keep it simple.

Grow at Home

God's Word tells us about the duty of parents to lead their children in worship. But this is not just a responsibility—it is a sacred privilege. Leading family worship in your home will bless your children and fill your home with God's grace and peace. As you begin, here are a few practical ideas that may help you make the most of your time of family worship. This section also contains several simple prayers and songs for you and your children to learn together.

Ideas to Make the Most of Your Time

1. Find a good children's Bible, such as *My First Bible, The Adventure Bible for Young Readers*, or

the *ESV Children's Bible*. Children love to have a Bible that they can call their own.

2. Have a daily time for family worship. Develop a routine for your children. Consistency is good for learning. It will show your children that this is an important part of the day.

3. Limit distractions. Make sure all screens are off.

4. Balance your time between Scripture memorization, using the catechism questions, and prayer and song. This book will help you bring those different areas together in a holistic approach to family discipleship.

5. Remember to have fun with your children while learning the Bible. Memorizing and learning about the Bible doesn't have to be boring. Make the time fun and special.

6. Keep the time brief to hold the children's attention.

7. Pray with your children every day at meals and before they go to bed at night. Let prayer become an important part of your home.

8. Share what you learn with other families. Encourage others to experience the blessings of doing faith together as a family.

9. Let your children ask questions and talk through what they are learning about God and the Bible.

One of the primary ways we learn is through communication.

10. Ask questions. After reading a Bible passage or catechism question, ask questions like, "What does this say about God?" or "How does God want me to respond?" Let your children ask questions that they may be thinking about.

Prayers for Family Worship

A Child's Grace

God is great and God is good,
And we thank God for our food;
By God's hand we must be fed,
Give us, Lord, our daily bread. Amen.

A Child's Prayer for Morning

Now, before I run to play,
Let me not forget to pray
To God who kept me through the night
And waked me with the morning light.
Help me, Lord, to love You more
Than I ever loved before.
In my work and in my play
Be with me through the day.
Amen.

God Hear My Prayer

God in heaven hear my prayer,
keep me in Your loving care.
Be my guide in all I do,
Bless all those who love me too.
Amen.

For Happy Hearts

We thank Thee, Lord, for happy hearts,
For rain and sunny weather.
We thank Thee, Lord, for this our food,
And that we are together.

Children's Bedtime Prayer

Now I lay me down to sleep,
I pray the Lord my soul to keep:
May God guard me through the night
And wake me with the morning light.
Amen

Songs for Family Worship

Jesus Loves Me

Jesus loves me! This I know,
For the Bible tells me so;
Little ones to Him belong;
They are weak, but He is strong.
Yes, Jesus loves me!
Yes, Jesus loves me!
Yes, Jesus loves me!
The Bible tells me so.

Jesus Loves the Little Children

Jesus loves the little children,
All the children of the world;
Red and yellow, black and white,
They are precious in his sight;
Jesus loves the little children of the world.

Jesus died for all the children,
All the children of the world;
Red and yellow, black and white,
They are precious in his sight;
Jesus died for all the little children of the world.

Jesus rose for all the children,
All the children of the world;
Red and yellow, black and white,
They are precious in his sight;
Jesus rose for all the little children of the world.

Jesus wants the little children,
To be careful what they do;
Honor father, mother dear,
Keep their hearts so full of cheer;
Then he'll take them home to glory by and by.

Books of the New Testament

Matthew, Mark, Luke, and John,
Acts and the letter to the Romans,
First and Second Corinthians, Galatians and
    Ephesians,
Philippians, Colossians, First and Second
    Thessalonians,
First and Second Timothy, Titus and Philemon,
Hebrews, James, First and Second Peter,
First and Second and Third John, Jude, and
    Revelation.

Chapter 3

Reading the Bible
as a Family

"Give them the Bible, the whole Bible, even while they are young."

—*J. C. Ryle*

The Bible was always meant to be read in community. There is a corporate dimension to reading the Scriptures that you don't get by reading it alone. The Old Testament was written for the people of Israel (see Deuteronomy 5 and 6; Nehemiah 8:6). The New Testament was written for Christians who gathered together in homes (see Acts 2:42). Therefore, it could rightly be said that the Bible isn't just for individuals, but for the people of God.

Many people, including myself, would say that the Bible is God's book for the family. Many of the books of the Bible were originally read aloud in a family setting where adults and children were gathered together. Think about it for a moment: most of the early church met in peoples' homes (see Acts 20:20; Romans 16:5; 1 Corinthians 16:19; Colossians 4:15; Philemon 1:2). I can imagine first-century Christian families sitting around together listening to the Bible being read aloud from pages freshly delivered from the hands of the apostles themselves. When we gather in the home to study the Bible together, we are doing the same thing that Christians have done since the time of Christ.

The Bible is God's holy Word given to us. As you read it every day, it will help your family mature and grow together spiritually. As you study the Bible it will strengthen your faith, speak to your heart, and guide you in all of life's tough decisions. As you continue to read the Bible, God will reveal His plans and purposes for your life. Take some time to see what God is trying to tell you from His Word. The Bible is one of the best ways for the Lord to speak to us.

Reading the Bible is very important for families to grow together. Jesus told his disciples, "If you abide in my word, you are truly my disciples, and you will know the truth, and the truth will set you free" (John 8:31–32). Families need to immerse themselves daily in God's Word, like the people who lived in Berea and who searched the Scriptures daily (see Acts 17:11).

Time and time again, my wife and I have gone to the Bible to find personal strength and encouragement for life's greatest challenges. Although the Bible isn't a question-and-answer book, it is the place where we learn about God's plan and purpose for our lives and for our families. The Bible offers foundations of faith for the family so that we can find answers to many of life's toughest questions.

What Is the Bible?

So what is the Bible? The Bible is a collection of many different books with a unified theme. As a whole, it is a massive work made up of sixty-six books, divided into the Old Testament and New Testament, and spans thousands of years. Together, the books paint a picture of God's redemptive plan for the world. They are ancient documents that have been preserved over time and were eventually translated into our language. To give you a better grasp of the story these books tell, I want to share what they are, and where they came from.

The Old Testament is made up of thirty-nine books, covering a two-thousand-year period beginning with the creation of the world, and closely recording the origins and history of the nation of Israel. However, it's not called the Old Testament because it's old, but because that testament reveals God's first covenant to humankind. A covenant is a special agreement between two parties that establishes a relationship based on mutual obligations and responsibilities. The old covenant refers to God's special relationship with the nation of Israel, which was based upon their obedience to God's law (see Genesis 17:1–19; Exodus 19–24).

The Old Testament includes history, poetry, and prophetic writings. It also contains some of the greatest stories ever told, such as the story of Moses and the Ten Commandments, Jonah in the belly of a whale, Daniel in the lions' den—and let's not forget the story of Samson and Delilah.

The New Testament is about Jesus Christ and is considerably smaller than the Old Testament; it has twenty-seven books. If you've never read God's Word, the New Testament is the place to start. Begin by reading the Gospels—the first four books of the New Testament—which tell about the life, ministry, message, death, and resurrection of Jesus.

Here you can find out more about Jesus' life and message for today. The Epistles are letters written to churches throughout the ancient Near Eastern world to address a variety of topics about the Christian life. The New Testament closes with the book of Revelation, which discusses futuristic events and the return of Christ.

Grow at Home

Reading the Bible as a family may seem a little overwhelming at first because it is absolutely massive and contains many different doctrines, characters, stories, and themes. The good news is that we don't have to be systematic theologians to read and understand God's Word. Reading the Bible is more like a marathon than a sprint, so I recommend that you start small. It will take a lifetime to study the entire Bible, and even then, you and I will never know all there is to know about it. Below are several suggestions that I would like to offer for getting the most from studying your Bible as a family.

The rest of this chapter offers simple scriptures to memorize with small children and then progresses to offer more advanced passages for older age levels. This is also ideal practice for parents who want to memorize along with their children. There is a place for you to date each step as your child memorizes a scripture. This will help you and your child chart their progress. At the end of this section is a list of Bible stories that you can look up and read with your children. These stories will capture their imagination and help them develop a love for the Bible even at a young age.

Reading the Bible Together

1. Read the Bible daily. There is no substitute for a regular study of Scripture. You would be surprised how much you and your children will gain from a daily study of the Bible.
2. Memorize scriptures. Begin with the following scriptures for memorization with your children. As you repeat the scriptures they will sink down into your heart and soul.
3. Recite a verse or question several times a day in your child's presence so it becomes familiar to them. It usually takes repeating something several times before you learn it.
4. You can make flash cards with Scripture on one side and the book, chapter, and verse on the other.
5. Put the verse to music or to a rhythm. Your child will enjoy singing and clapping their hands.

6. Think of activities to make the verse fun and easy to remember. Be creative. Specialize your learning time in a way that is unique to you and your child.

7. Reward your child when he/she has memorized a verse. Rewards could include small treats or prizes, a trip to the store, or special time with mom or dad.

8. Tell them you are proud of them and have them recite it to someone else like a grandparent or teacher. Children love to share what they have learned.

9. Date each step as your child memorizes a scripture or one of the catechism questions. This will help you and your child chart their progress.

10. Lastly, share what you learn in the Bible with others in your family. Teaching is one of the best ways to reinforce what you have learned. Let your children be the teachers as well as the students.

Scriptures for Memorization

Genesis 1:1: In the beginning, God created the heavens and the earth.

Date_____

Psalm 118:24: This is the day the LORD has made; let us rejoice and be glad in it.

Date_____

Psalm 119:105: Your word is a lamp to my feet and a light to my path.

Date_____

Psalm 136:1: Give thanks to the LORD, for he is good.

Date_____

Luke 6:31: And as you wish that others would do to you, do so to them.

Date_____

Philippians 4:13: I can do all things through him who strengthens me.

Date_____

Psalm 23:1: The LORD is my shepherd; I shall not want.

Date_____

John 3:16: For God so loved the world, that he gave his only Son.

Date_____

John 8:12: Jesus spoke to them, saying, "I am the light of the world."
Date_____

Matthew 22:37: You shall love the Lord your God with all your heart and with all your soul and with all your mind.
Date_____

Matthew 22:39: You shall love your neighbor as yourself.
Date_____

Ephesians 6:1: Children, obey your parents in the Lord, for this is right.
Date_____

1 Peter 5:7: [Cast] all your anxieties on him, because he cares for you.
Date_____

Psalm 19:14: Let the words of my mouth and the meditation of my heart be acceptable in your sight, O Lord, my rock and my redeemer.
Date_____

Psalm 139:14: I praise you, for I am fearfully and wonderfully made. Wonderful are your works; my soul knows it very well.

Date_____

Matthew 1:21: She will bear a son, and you shall call his name Jesus, for he will save his people from their sins.

Date_____

Matthew 28:19: Go therefore and make disciples of all nations, baptizing them in the name of the Father and of the Son and of the Holy Spirit.

Date_____

John 1:1–2: In the beginning was the Word, and the Word was with God, and the Word was God. He was in the beginning with God.

Date_____

John 14:1: Let not your hearts be troubled. Believe in God; believe also in me.

Date_____

Ephesians 4:32: Be kind to one another, tender-hearted, forgiving one another, as God in Christ forgave you.
Date_____

Psalm 19:1: The heavens declare the glory of God, and the sky above proclaims his handiwork.
Date_____

1 John 4:7: Let us love one another, for love is from God, and whoever loves has been born of God and knows God.
Date_____

Proverbs 3:5–6: Trust in the LORD with all your heart, and do not lean on your own understanding. In all your ways acknowledge him, and he will make straight your paths.
Date_____

Isaiah 40:31: But they who wait for the Lord shall renew their strength; they shall mount up with wings like eagles; they shall run and not be weary; they shall walk and not faint.
Date_____

Matthew 7:7–8: Ask, and it will be given to you; seek, and you will find; knock, and it will be opened to you.
Date_____

John 10:14: I am the good shepherd. I know my own and my own know me.
Date_____

1 John 1:9: If we confess our sins, he is faithful and just to forgive us our sins and to cleanse us from all unrighteousness.
Date_____

The Ten Commandments

1. You shall have no other gods before me.
2. You shall not make for yourself any carved image.
3. You shall not take the LORD's name in vain.
4. Remember the Sabbath and keep it holy.
5. Honor your father and mother.
6. You shall not commit murder.
7. You shall not commit adultery.
8. You shall not steal.
9. You shall not bear false witness.
10. You shall not covet.

Date_____

The Twelve Disciples

Simon Peter

Andrew

James

John

Philip

Thomas

Matthew

James the son of Alphaeus

Thaddaeus

Simon

Judas

Bartholomew

Date_____

Bible Stories

Creation	Genesis 1–2
Adam and Eve	Genesis 1–3
Noah and the flood	Genesis 6–9
Promise to Abraham	Genesis 12, 18, 21
God cares for Joseph	Genesis 37, 39–47
A baby called Moses	Exodus 1–2
Samson	Judges 13–16
David and Goliath	1 Samuel 17
Daniel in lion's den	Daniel 1–2, 6
Birth of Jesus	Luke 2:1–20

Chapter 4

Teaching Children Truths through Catechism

"I am persuaded that the use of a good Catechism in all our families will be a great safeguard against the increasing errors of the times."

—*Charles Spurgeon*

Do you remember the show called *Kids Say the Darndest Things*? In a similar way, my children have taught me that kids also *ask* the darndest things. Our seven-year-old daughter Anna Belle loves to ask questions. She has a knack for asking particularly tough questions that are not easy to answer. In fact, this afternoon she asked me, "If our house was burning down and the fire department came to help, would we have to pay them for coming?" The truth is, I don't really know!

Questions are an important part of life. You are never too old or too young to ask questions. When you're growing up, you don't know all of the answers. In fact, you typically have a lot more questions than you do answers. That's why children ask so many. Questions like "How can birds fly?" or "Where do people go when they die?" or "Why does the sun set and rise?" or "Where is heaven?" I could go on.

Questions are natural ways to find out the basic answers to life. Questions are also an essential part of growing in your faith. They help us discover the mysteries of our faith. They are how we learn, grow, and ultimately come to believe. Once you stop asking questions, you stop learning, growing, and believing.

Learning through Questions and Answers

Christians throughout the ages have used simple questions and answers to teach the faith to children. Over time, Christians began to put questions and answers down in a formal teaching method called a catechism. The Greek word for "instruct" or "teach" is *katecheo*, from which we get our English word "catechize." Catechesis is the process of instructing children and adults in the basic essentials of the Christian faith.

Catechisms are basic summaries of the church's teachings to ensure that all members of the church understand the essentials of the faith for themselves using a question-and-answer format. Catechisms are not a pass or fail fill-in-the-blank test, but an invitation to learn the doctrines of grace. Using a catechism involves vital learning, ongoing reflection, and discussion within the community of faith.

Catechisms have been used by Christians for centuries. As early as Augustine (AD 353–430), the Christian church has used catechisms to instruct new believers. During the time of the Protestant Reformation, the Reformers compiled many catechisms to help train new believers.

The Puritans also developed catechisms for their day. Puritan pastors encouraged heads of families to catechize family members in their home. Richard Baxter said, "Persuade the master of every family to cause his children and servants to repeat the Catechism to him, every Sabbath evening, and to give him some account of what they have heard at church during the day."[1] Puritan pastors regularly visited the homes of their flock to catechize families. The Puritans believed that the parents had a personal responsibility to catechize their family members.

The Foundation of the Creeds

Many of the historic catechisms were primarily built on the foundation of the early Christian creeds: the Apostles' and Nicene. A creed is a brief statement of faith used to clarify doctrinal points and to distinguish truth from error. The word "creed" comes from the Latin word *credo*, meaning "I believe." The Bible contains a number of creed-like passages (see Deuteronomy 6:4–9; 1 Corinthians 8:6; 12:3; 15:3–4; 1 Timothy 3:16). The creeds offer us a concise summary of authentic Christian doctrine.

As the early church spread, there was a practical need for a statement of faith to help believers focus on the most important doctrines of their Christian faith. The Apostles' Creed is named not because the original apostles wrote it, but because it accurately reflects the teaching of the apostles. The final text of the Apostles' Creed was eventually accepted around 800 AD as the standard form in the Western church.[2]

As the church continued to grow, heresies also grew, and the early Christians needed to clarify the defining boundaries of the faith. In the early 300s, controversy developed over the divinity of Jesus Christ. At the request of Emperor Constantine, Christian bishops from across the East and the West met at the town of Nicea, near Constantinople. In 325 AD they wrote an expanded creed, called the Creed of Nicea. These two creeds are widely accepted among all Christians as statements of true Christian orthodoxy. In particular, the Apostles' Creed has been used for memorization and catechizing children.

Catechisms Today

Today, there is a misconception that catechisms are a thing of the past. You may be thinking to yourself, "Why use catechisms for my children? Aren't they outdated or irrelevant in the postmodern world? Kids are too young to start learning about doctrine." The truth is that children are never too young to learn about their faith. Many times I don't think we, as parents, take our children seriously enough. They are more intelligent than we give them credit for. Catechisms are a time-tested way to teach children about our faith by using simple questions and answers.

Catechisms are good for both parents and children alike. They are a simple way that you can teach and learn basic Christian doctrine with your children. Catechisms were originally developed to be used to help children and adults alike grasp the essentials of the Christian faith. Therefore, a catechism is a wonderful way for you and your children to explore Christian truth together as a family.

Grow at Home

Here is family catechism with forty questions in modern English that you can use with your children in the home. This catechism is also ideal for a confirmation class or for youth who are preparing to be baptized. The questions can be adapted for various ages and you can feel free to edit or omit the questions as necessary depending on the age of your children. You may use the catechism in the morning, evening, at the dinner table, or whenever best fits your family's needs. When using the catechism questions, allow time for your children to ponder each question and reflect on the answers. It's okay if they ask more in-depth questions.

For a more structured way to use the catechism, you can divide up the questions into four-week sessions. Study the set of questions with your children once a day for a week and then offer them a test at the end of the week to see how well they have learned the answers. Whenever they are ready, move on to the next set of questions.

At the end of the catechism questions you will find two creeds. First is the Apostles' Creed, which is broken into three parts to make it easier to learn and memorize. I have also included a shorter affirmation of the faith based upon the historic creeds for smaller children.

Week 1: The Bible, God, and Jesus (Questions 1–13)

Week 2: Salvation and Grace (Questions 14–22)

Week 3: The Spirit and the Church (Questions 23–32)

Week 4: The Commandments and Prayer (Questions 33–40)

Family Catechism

1. Q. What is the Bible?
   A. The Bible is the story of God's love for lost humankind.

2. Q. What is the Old Testament?

   A. The Old Testament begins with the creation of the world and records the history of the nation of Israel.

3. Q. What is the New Testament?

   A. The New Testament tells us about the life and teachings of Jesus and the good news of the kingdom.

4. Q. Who wrote the Bible?

   A. The Holy Spirit inspired men of faith to write the Bible.

5. Q. Who is God?

   A. God is our heavenly Father.

6. Q. What does it mean that God is the Father Almighty?

   A. God loves us as a father loves his children.

7. Q. What does it mean that God is Creator?

   A. God created the universe and everything in it, including you and me.

8. Q. What is our response to God?

   A. We are to worship God and God alone.

9. Q. Who is Jesus Christ?

   A. Jesus is the Son of God our Lord.

10. Q. What do we mean when we say that Jesus was conceived by the power of the Holy Spirit and born of the Virgin Mary?

A. We mean that Jesus Christ is fully God and fully man.

11. Q. Why did Jesus suffer and die on a cross?
A. Jesus died on the cross to set us free from the power of sin and to reconcile us to God.

12. Q. What is the significance of Jesus' resurrection?
A. By His resurrection, Jesus rose from the grave and overcame death and opened for us the way of eternal life.

13. Q. Where is Jesus now?
A. Jesus is in heaven where He now reigns with the Father and intercedes for us.

14. Q. What is sin?
A. Sin is the seeking of our own will instead of the will of God.

15. Q. What are we saved from?
A. We are saved from sin and death by grace through faith in God.

16. Q. What is grace?
A. Grace is God's love freely given to us.

17. Q. What must we do to be saved?
A. We must repent of our sins and accept Jesus as our Lord and Savior.

18. Q. What does it mean to repent?
A. To repent means to turn from our sin to God in order to live a new life of obedience to Christ.

19. Q. What is the gospel?

A. The gospel is the good news that Jesus Christ died for our sins on the cross in order to set us free from the power of sin and death.

20. Q. What do we mean by the resurrection of the body?

A. God will raise us from death in the fullness of our being, that we may live with Christ forever.

21. Q. What do we mean by everlasting life?

A. We will live with God forever.

22. Q. What is our assurance as Christians?

A. Our assurance as Christians is that nothing, not even death, shall separate us from the love of God, which is in Christ Jesus our Lord.

23. Q. Who is the Holy Spirit?

A. The Holy Spirit is the third person of the Trinity, God at work in the world and in the church even now.

24. Q. What is the Trinity?

A. The Trinity is one God: Father, Son, and Holy Spirit.

25. Q. What does the Holy Spirit do in our life?

A. The Holy Spirit baptizes every believer into the body of Christ and bestows upon us spiritual gifts.

26. Q. What is the church?

A. The church is the body of Jesus Christ and we are members of His body.

27. Q. How many sacraments are there?

A. There are two sacraments: baptism and the Lord's Supper.

28. Q. What is baptism?

A. Baptism is when a person is baptized in water in the name of the Father, and of the Son, and of the Holy Spirit.

29. Q. What is the inward and spiritual grace in baptism?

A. The inward and spiritual grace in baptism is forgiveness of sins and new life in Christ.

30. Q. What is required of us at baptism?

A. It is required that we repent of our sins and accept Jesus as our Lord and Savior.

31. Q. What is the Lord's Supper?

A. The Lord's Supper is a continual remembrance of Jesus' life, death, and resurrection.

32. Q. What is the outward and visible sign in the Lord's Supper?

A. The bread and cup are symbolic of the body and blood of Christ.

33. Q. What are the Ten Commandments?

A. The Ten Commandments are God's laws, given to Moses and the people of Israel.

34. Q. What do we learn from these commandments?
    A. We learn two things: our duty to God and our duty to our neighbors.

35. Q. What is our duty to God?
    A. Our duty is to believe and trust in God.

36. Q. What is our duty to our neighbors?
    A. Our duty to our neighbors is to love them as ourselves and to do to other people as we wish them to do to us.

37. Q. What is the summary of the Law?
    A. You shall love the Lord your God with all your heart, with all your soul, and with all your mind. This is the first and great commandment. And the second is like it: you shall love your neighbor as yourself.

38. Q. What is the New Commandment?
    A. The New Commandment is that we love one another as Christ loved us.

39. Q. What is prayer?
    A. Prayer is talking to God, which includes praise, confession, thanksgiving, and asking requests in the name of Jesus Christ.

40. Q. What prayer did Christ teach us?
    A. Our Lord gave us the example of prayer known as the Lord's Prayer.

The Apostles' Creed

I believe in God, the Father almighty,
creator of heaven and earth;

I believe in Jesus Christ, his only Son, our Lord.
He was conceived by the power of the Holy Spirit
 and born of the Virgin Mary.
He suffered under Pontius Pilate,
was crucified, died, and was buried.
He descended to the dead.
 On the third day he rose again.
He ascended into heaven,
and is seated at the right hand of the Father.
He will come again to judge the living and the dead.

I believe in the Holy Spirit,
the holy catholic Church,[3]
the communion of saints,
the forgiveness of sins
the resurrection of the body,
and the life everlasting. *Amen.*

Affirmation of the Faith

We believe in God the Father, Almighty.
We believe in Jesus Christ, His Only Son.
We believe in the Holy Spirit, Giver of Life.
We believe in the Three in One. *Amen.*

Chapter 5

Cultivating Character through the Fruits of the Spirit

"It is not education, accomplishments, material possessions, health, or significance. It is character that will sustain a child, an adult, a family."
—John Yates

Our culture idolizes people based on their fame and fortune, rather than their character or morals. Is it any wonder that there is a crisis of character? In North America, superstars are usually the ones who influence our youth the most. All you have to do is watch the latest television program or listen to songs that are geared for children and teens. Sadly, children are the ones who are most affected by the world's lack of morality. If we are not careful we will let the television and media shape and mold our children into what the world says they should be like.

This raises the question, "Who and what shapes our children's character and morals?" Is it the school? Is it television? Is it the government? The answer should be *no!*

As parents, we are the ones who have been given the divine responsibility to help shape our children's character. The Bible tells us to "Train up a child in the way he should go; even when he is old he will not depart from it" (Prov. 22:6). John and Susan Yates remind us, "Parents are the fundamental key to the development of their children's character."[1]

The character development of our children is the sacred responsibility of every parent. As we seek to cultivate character in our children, we must turn again and again to the well-worn pages of the Bible. As Christians, our character should be shaped by the Bible, rather than our culture. The Bible is full of principles by which we can live and shape our lives. We have been given a treasure chest of great tools in the Bible to help us train our children in the ways of God.

Learning to Live in the Spirit

Parenting can seem overwhelming at times. However, the good news is that we are not alone in this great task. God partners with us in the character development of children. He gives us His Holy Spirit to lead and guide us. Jesus said, "When the Spirit of truth comes, he will guide you into all the truth" (John 16:13). The Holy Spirit wants to give us the wisdom, guidance, and direction that we need to raise our children in the faith. The Spirit wants to be our guide as we seek to help our children grow.

I would like to share with you one of the most helpful ways that my wife and I have found to help teach our children biblical principles of character. It is the fruits of the Spirit (see Galatians 5:16, 22, 25). The fruits of the Spirit are nine Christ-like qualities that the Holy Spirit imparts to believers as they walk with Him. They are the hallmark of a Spirit-filled life and the direct result of the Spirit's work in and through us.

According to Paul, the fruits of the Spirit are a natural result of "walk[ing] by the Spirit" (Gal. 5:16). As a farmer prepares for a harvest of fruit, the

Spirit cultivates the fruits of the Spirit in the life of believers. As we yield ourselves to the Holy Spirit, we are liberated to experience His fullness in our lives and in our homes. The result of the fruits of the Spirit in our lives is Christ-like character. All we have to do is surrender our hearts and our lives to Him daily.

As a family, we found that the work of the Spirit is essential to character development. We memorized the fruits of the Spirit together and seek to use them as a model for character development in our home and in our children's lives. Once we learned them together, we were able to use them as a model of Christ's work in us through the Holy Spirit in our daily lives. This has been especially helpful when it comes to discipline in the home. Here is an overview of each of the fruits of the Spirit that Paul mentions.

Love

The first and most important fruit of the Spirit is love. Love is the virtue of brotherly and sacrificial love. It is a love that seeks the good of others. Paul's order of placement for the word "love" tells us that it is the greatest of the fruits (see 1 Corinthians 13; Ephesians 5:2; Colossians 3:14). Other New

Testament writers, such as John and Peter, emphasize love as one of the greatest features of the kingdom of God.

Love is a spiritual anchor of truth in relationship with God and neighbor. This love is a distinctly Christian love, which finds its source from God alone. Because of this kind of love, God sent His only Son to die for us. The Holy Spirit is hard at work to reproduce this kind of love in each one of us. We are to show this kind of selfless love to one another and to the world.

Joy

The second fruit of the Spirit is joy. The word joy appears sixty times in the New Testament. Joy corresponds to happiness, but it is independent of outward circumstances and is to be found within every believer's life. Joy is a deep gladness that comes from a personal relationship with Jesus Christ.

As Christians, everything that we do should be done with joy in our hearts. The Bible tells us that we are to serve the Lord with joy and gladness. God desires for His children to know the joy of the Lord. The Bible says that the joy of the Lord is our strength (see Nehemiah 8:10). Let the Holy Spirit fill you with joy today as you serve Him.

Peace

Peace is the third fruit of the Spirit. Peace refers to a tranquility of mind, body, and soul. It is a spiritual well-being that only God can give a person. Nations might be able to produce a world of peace, but God is the only one who can offer total peace. Jesus said, "Peace I leave with you; my peace I give to you. Not as the world gives do I give to you. Let not your hearts be troubled, neither let them be afraid" (John 14:27). God's peace will never pass away. In fact, Paul calls it the peace that surpasses all understanding (see Philippians 4:7). This doesn't mean that you will never have another problem, but that God will give you peace in the midst of the storm. Let the peace of God fill your heart and soul through the power of the Spirit.

Long-Suffering

Long-suffering is the fourth fruit of the Spirit. The Greek word is commonly translated "patience" but the King James Version renders a more accurate translation of the word "long-suffering." The verb means to place or arrange under for a long time. Christians should be able to hold strong in the midst of trials and difficulty.

We need to be steadfast and endure. This means waiting through the difficult times, even when we are severely tried, confused, or weak. It is like being a spiritual rubber band. When we are being stretched we will not break if we have long-suffering. The Holy Spirit will supernaturally give us patience to hold on under difficult situations and circumstances.

Kindness

The fifth fruit of the Spirit is sympathetic kindness. It is God's virtuous gift to be able to respond to the special needs of others who are hurting or in need. It is a quality of God's kindness that is found in the New Testament only in Paul's correspondence.

Those who have experienced the kindness of God's salvation in Christ are to clothe themselves with the same kindness. In a world full of anger, selfishness, and contention, the Lord wants us to cultivate the fruit of kindness in our lives. Let the Lord use you to show kindness to others.

Goodness

The sixth fruit of the Spirit is goodness. Goodness is the generosity that overflows from kindness. Although goodness and kindness are similar, good-ness is a more active term, which is often directed toward others in a benevolent way. It is the action of helping others in need. We are to take action and become agents of God's goodness in the world. When we see a need we must meet it. When we see a hurt we must heal it. The virtue of goodness reminds us that we become the hands and feet of Jesus Christ. The Holy Spirit desires to use us as vehicles through which the goodness of God may flow.

Faithfulness

This is one of the most common words in the New Testament. It is used in a variety of ways to mean faith, but considering the ethical context of Galatians, the word is accurately translated "faithfulness." It refers to being a person that others can rely upon. You cannot have faith in God without being faithful. The two are one in the same. The Spirit of the Lord wants to make us responsible persons in every area of our lives. As you think about the word "faithfulness," ask yourself the question, "Can God trust me to be faithful?"

Gentleness

The eighth fruit of the Spirit is gentleness. It literally means to be mild or tame. The word is often used to refer to an animal, such as a bridled horse. In the personal sense it refers more to controlled strength than it does weakness. Gentleness isn't a sign of weakness, instead is it a sign of the Spirit's strength in us and through us.

Gentleness is closely associated to the word humility. Jesus Christ is our great example of gentleness and humility. Being God, He humbled himself to becoming one of us (see Philippians 2). Gentleness is the virtue that is needed when confronted by opposition and persecution. Peter tells us that gentleness is necessary to have a genuine witness (see 1 Peter 3:15–16). Without gentleness we cannot be a true Christian witness to the world.

Self-Control

The final ethical virtue of the Spirit is self-control, or temperance. It is victory over the desires of the flesh. It is the virtue of a person who masters their passions and desires. It is opposite to the desires of the flesh. Self-control is closely associated to purity of mind, heart, and conduct. It is the ability to crucify the flesh and walk in the Spirit. It is relying on the power of the Spirit to overcome the desires of the flesh. We need more self-control in our daily lives.

Grow at Home

The fruits of the Spirit are an excellent way for you to teach your children Christ-like character in the home. Each fruit can be used as a devotional thought for the day or week. Take time to study and learn each one of them and to memorize them with your children.

The Fruits of the Spirit

1. Love
2. Joy
3. Peace
4. Patience
5. Kindness
6. Goodness
7. Faithfulness
8. Gentleness
9. Self-Control

Chapter 6

Learning to Pray the Lord's Prayer

"'Our Father:'—If he is a Father, then he is good, then he is loving, to his children."
                                        —John Wesley

The disciples asked Jesus, "Lord teach us how to pray." If you think about it for a moment, they could have asked him anything in the world but they chose to ask him about prayer. It was because they knew that he had a powerful prayer life and deep devotion to his heavenly Father.

Jesus was the greatest example of prayer. Prayer wasn't just a message that Jesus preached, but the life that he lived.[1] In between preaching to thousands of people, performing miracles, feeding multitudes, and healing the sick, Jesus still managed to find time to pray in secret. The Gospels tell us that Jesus prayed at every major event in His life: His baptism (Luke 3:21); the choice of apostles (6:12–12); His transfiguration (9:29); before the cross at Gethsemane (22:39–40); and on the cross (23:46). Even now, the Bible tells us that He continues in prayer for us. Hebrews 7:25 says, "He always lives to make intercessions for them." He sets the example of prayer for us to follow.

The secret to Jesus' powerful prayer life is found in the most important prayer of the Bible, commonly known as "the Lord's Prayer." The Lord's Prayer is the most universally and best-known Christian prayer of all time. It is read at funerals, weddings, and church services throughout the Christian world. Two versions of it occur in the New Testament, one in Matthew 6:9–13 and the other in Luke 11:2–4. The Lord's Prayer is also known as the "Our Father." It contains the heart of Jesus' teaching on prayer, and offers us an outline by which we can shape our own personal prayer life and learn to pray according to His will.

The Lord's Prayer is a powerful model prayer for families to learn together. It can help shape our personal and family prayer life. A great way to teach your children the Lord's Prayer is by reciting it every day. Children learn by repetition. In our home, we pray the Lord's Prayer together at dinner and before bed every evening. Many times, our girls will lead us in saying the Lord's Prayer. Our church has also embraced the Lord's Prayer on Sunday mornings by praying it after our time of song worship. Then, our children are also encouraged to pray it together during Sunday school.

Our Father in Heaven

There are several important things to look at when examining the Lord's Prayer and applying it to our family prayer life. The Lord's Prayer begins with acknowledging that God is our heavenly Father. So many people think that prayer is about them, but Jesus reminds us that prayer begins with God, His kingdom, and His ways. True prayer is putting God first and seeking first the kingdom and His righteousness for our lives. Everything else flows from this foundation.

Knowing that God is our heavenly Father affects how we pray. We are not praying to some abstract being in outer space, but our heavenly Father. Think about that for a minute. He is our loving Father! The Lord's Prayer reminds us of who He is and who we are. God is our heavenly Father, and we are His children. As our Father, He loves us and wants to take care of us, and we can come to Him in prayer whenever we need to.

His Name Is Holy

The second petition of the Lord's Prayer is "Hallowed be your name." To hallow means "to make holy." The second part of the prayer is to glorify God's name through praise and worship. In other words, prayer is an act of divine worship that begins by acknowledging God for who He is and praising Him for His mighty acts and greatness. Worship takes our eyes off of ourselves and our problems and puts our focus back onto God and His kingdom. Beginning prayer by offering worship to God helps us keep the proper perspective on prayer.

His Kingdom and His Will

The purpose of our prayer should be to pray for His kingdom to come and His will to be done. Jesus Himself told the Father, "not my will but your will be done." Prayer is not just coming to God with our own personal agenda; rather it is seeking His agenda for our life and His will. His ways are greater than our ways and His plan is always better than our plans. Sometimes we have to learn this the hard way.

Prayer is asking for God's will. God is not a Santa Claus; He does not give us anything we ask for or everything we want. The reason is simple: God knows what we need not just what we want. We need to distinguish between our wants and needs. Many times the things that we want are not what we need and the things we need are not what we want. One of the reasons why we need to seek His will is our Father knows what is best for us. This is why the Lord's Prayer says, "Thy will be done on earth as it is in heaven." His will must always come before our will.

One of the best ways to pray for God's will is to pray according to the Scriptures. John 15:7 says, "If you abide in me, and my word abides in you, ask whatever you wish, and it will be done for you." If God's Word is in us then His desires become our desires and we can have the assurance that He hears our prayers. Make sure that your prayers are in line with Scripture because the Lord always honors His Word. A great example of praying according to the Scriptures is reading through the psalms or using the Lord's Prayer as a model.

His Provision

The next petition is "give us this day our daily bread." An important part of prayer is asking God to meet your needs. We should not be afraid to ask the Lord to meet our basic needs because in doing so we acknowledge that He is Lord over our lives and everything that we are and everything that we have comes from Him. Jesus isn't talking about praying for cars and material things, but our basic needs, our "daily bread."

This prayer should help us overcome our anxieties about life and the future. Many people live in fear of losing their job, their house, or their 401k. We need to understand that it is God's desire to take care of His children. Philippians 4:19 says, "My God will supply every need of yours according to his riches in glory in Christ Jesus." Whatever your needs are, don't be afraid to ask God to help you with them today and trust that He will hear your prayer. The Bible says, "Do not be anxious about anything, but in everything by prayer and supplication with thanksgiving let your request be made known to God" (Phil. 4:6). A supplication is a specific request to God for specific things. Don't be afraid to ask the Lord in prayer; remember He is your Father. I suggest having a prayer journal so that you will be able to keep track of what to pray for and when God answers your prayers.

His Forgiveness

The next petition is "Forgive us our debts." No one is perfect, especially me. I need God's grace and forgiveness every day. Some days I need it more than others. We are broken, fallen, sinful people who desperately need the forgiveness of God. The Lord's Prayer reminds us that we are able to come before a holy and just God and confess our sins and receive forgiveness. The Bible says that "he is faithful and just to forgive us our sins and to cleanse us from all unrighteousness" (1 John 1:9). It's important to remind ourselves that forgiveness isn't just for the lost, but for Christians too.

Not only do we need to receive forgiveness for ourselves, but we need to give it away, too. We should freely forgive others as God has freely forgiven us. Jesus gives a significant attention on the importance of forgiving others, "For if you forgive others their trespasses, your heavenly Father will also forgive you, but if you do not forgive others their trespasses, neither will your Father forgive your trespasses" (Matt. 6:14–15). God wants to bring healing and restoration to broken relationships. Earlier in Matthew 5:21–26, Jesus warns us that if we have something against a brother we need to go and be reconciled.

His Protection

The sixth and seventh petitions are "Lead us not into temptation, but deliver us from the evil one." Temptation and spiritual warfare are realities of the Christian life that we face every day. Therefore, we need God's help to protect us and give us strength to face these battles. Every day brings with it new challenges and new battles, but the good news is that God is with us. This reminds us that He is not absent or disengaged, but ever present help in time of trouble.

The Bible tells us that we are in the midst of a spiritual battle and our adversary, the devil, is like a roaring lion seeking to destroy our lives. Paul says, "For we do not wrestle against flesh and blood, but against the rulers, against the authorities, against the cosmic powers over this present darkness, against the spiritual forces of evil in the heavenly places" (Eph. 6:12). Are you facing temptations, struggles, battles from within or the outside? Don't grow weary or give up but allow the Lord to help you pray for victory in every area of your life.

His Power

The Lord's Prayer closes in a way similar to how it started, by acknowledging God's greatness: "For yours is the kingdom and the power and the glory." The prayer ends in a doxology and praise to God and call for us to savor in God's kingdom and His glory. We are so consumed with our plans and busy lives we no longer live in amazement of God's splendor and greatness. The Bible tells us "be still, and know that I am God" (Ps. 46:10). We need to stop to take time to reflect on God's greatness in our lives.

I have lived for ten years in the Outer Banks, which is a beautiful stretch of islands on the coast of North Carolina. We have some of the most amazing sunrises and sunsets. Usually I don't take the time to stop and watch the sunset, but I remember one evening when I took the time to pull my car over to marvel at God's glory and watch an amazing red sunset go down into the ocean. Tears came to my eyes as I thought about God's greatness. When is the last time you took a moment as a family to pause and reflect on God's greatness?

Grow at Home

Take some time and memorize the Lord's Prayer together as a family. Start by praying it together each day. It may take you a few days or even a couple of weeks to learn the prayer by heart. The sad thing is that the Lord's Prayer is just words for some people. Don't let it be dead words, but a living tradition that you pray from the heart. As you go through the Lord's Prayer, reflect on what each line means. As you go, begin to pray it from the heart as a family several times a day. You can write it on note cards or post it on places like the refrigerator. As you pray as a family, ask your children to help lead in praying. Here are two versions of the prayer that you can memorize with your children.

Traditional Version

Our Father in heaven,
Hallowed be Thy name.
Thy kingdom come
Thy will be done
On earth as it is in heaven.
Give us this day our daily bread.
And forgive us our trespasses,
As we forgive those who trespass against us.

And lead us not into temptation,
but deliver us from the evil one.
For Thine is the kingdom,
and the power
and the glory forever, Amen.

Contemporary Version

Our Father in heaven,
holy is Your name.
Your kingdom come.
Your will be done
on earth as it is in heaven.
Give us this day our daily bread,
and forgive us our sins,
as we forgive those who sin against us,
and lead us not into temptation,
but deliver us from evil.
For Yours is the kingdom,
and the power, and the glory,
for ever and ever. Amen.

Chapter 7

Becoming a Missional Family

"My job as a parent is not only to teach my children these are the things you're supposed to do, but teach my children that they're supposed to be a part of God's mission as well."
—*Paul Tripp*

Mission is the duty of every Christian believer, young and old. We are all called to be missional Christians who share the good news of Jesus' love and forgiveness with the world. So what does it mean to be missional? Ed Stetzer wrote, "Being Missional means actually doing mission right where you are. Missional means adopting the posture of a missionary, learning and adapting to the culture around you while remaining biblically sound."[1]

Not only are we called to be missional as individuals, but also as families. God never intended for us to do mission alone. Every family can be missional together. Your family can be missional; the key is to teach mission to your children and then be intentional about creating opportunities to be missional together. This chapter will explore what it means to be a missional family and will offer some ideas and suggestions to help you live out God's mission in your family.

Mission Begins with Jesus

Being missional doesn't begin with us, it begins with Jesus Christ. Jesus Christ was the first and greatest missionary. The Bible tells us that He came from heaven to earth to die for a lost and dying world. As the Father sent Jesus, He also sends us into our time and culture. We have been chosen by God to live in this time and place in order to fulfill the mission of God.

Acts 17:26–27 tells us that God has determined the exact place and time where we should live so that men may find him. That means that the Lord planted your family exactly where you live for a reason: mission. It is truly awesome to realize that you have been chosen by God to be his missionaries to this world. It is both a great privilege and great responsibility. Paul describes our calling in the following way: "Therefore, we are ambassadors for Christ, God making his appeal through us. We implore you on behalf of Christ, be reconciled to God" (2 Cor. 5:20).

Being missional is God's way of showing the love of His Son Jesus through the lives of His followers. Being missional is striving to live like Jesus, our perfect example. Jesus said, "For even the Son of Man came not to be served but to serve, and to give his life as a ransom for many" (Mark 10:45). This scripture beautifully embodies what it means to be missional. To be missional is to serve and give our lives for others.

Sharing Our Faith Together

There are two primary ways that we can become missional families. The first way to be a missional family is by sharing the gospel message with others through our words. Sharing our faith is the duty of every believer, both young and old. We can share our faith together as a family. After all, Jesus sent his disciples out two by two. There are no lone rangers in the kingdom of God.

The ancient Celtic Christians did mission as a team instead of individually. They didn't go out and try to win the world by themselves, rather they went out as a team because they understood the power of community. Each member played an important role in the whole of reaching the community. Author John Finney observed that the Celts believed in "the importance of the team. A group of people can pray and think together. They inspire and encourage each other. The single entrepreneur is too easily prey to self doubt and loss of vision."[2] The Celtic approach to evangelism is an important alternative to the modern "lone ranger" approach that is typical in so many Western churches.

One of the most powerful witnesses that we can offer the world is by living out our faith together as a family. If you think about it, most non-Christians have no idea what it means to be a Christian family. They will not know the difference unless they see it in our families. Jesus said, "By this all people will know that you are my disciples, if you have love for one another" (John 13:35). The love that we share and the way we discipline our children is a powerful witness to the world. The world desperately needs to know and see what a Christ-centered family looks like.

Sometimes, our children will be the ones to lead the way. A few years ago we had some neighbors whom I had written off; I never thought they would come to faith. Then, one day my daughter invited them to come to church, and much to my surprise they came. I must admit I felt a little foolish when I ended up baptizing the young mother after she became a Christian.

Sharing our faith with others can begin in family prayer before we ever leave our house. You can pray with your children for your unchurched family, friends, and neighbors. Simply pray that God will give you the right opportunity and the right words to say. Pray that God would open up the hearts and minds of the unchurched people that He sends in your path. You would be surprised how many opportunities God will open up for you to share your faith with others if we simply stopped to pray. The Holy Spirit will open the hearts and the doors when the time is right. I can think of many times we have had a chance to share the gospel with other parents in the park, over a meal, or at the beach.

Meeting Needs

The second way of being a missional family is by helping to meet the needs of others. Jesus met both the spiritual and physical needs of the people He ministered to. He not only preached to the people, but He fed them too. It is universally true that people don't care how much you know till they know how much you care.

Every day in the United Sates, there are literally millions of people who are living in poverty in the shadow of our nation's great wealth. Hunger and poverty are quickly becoming a serious epidemic in the United States. There are many people in every city of our nation who are homeless and can't even provide for their own basic needs, such as food and clothing. In addition, drugs, domestic violence, and illiteracy are harsh realities for many people.

These people are not numbers or mere statistics, but they have names, faces, and feelings. More important, they have real needs that can be helped by believers. They are in our cities, communities, and small towns. They are our neighbors, fellow church members, and even family members.

God is concerned about the needy, destitute, hurting, poor, and orphans of the world. The Word tells us that we are commissioned to care for those around us who cannot care for themselves. Too long we've tried to stick Band-Aids on wounds that will not heal overnight. Being missional is going into places where the world doesn't want to go. Being missional can be very dirty. If we are going to make a difference we must roll up our sleeves and join in the work of Jesus among the poor and disenfranchised of this world.

In Our Own Backyards

Being a missional family starts in our own backyard. Find the needs of your community and begin to fill them by being a missionary to your city and community. We will never know what the needs of our community are until we begin to get outside the four walls of our house. It is amazing how little Christians actually interact with non-churchgoers. Matthew 9:35 tells us that when Jesus went out into all the cities and villages, He saw that the multitudes were weary and had compassion on them. As Jesus went into the community, He saw the needs of the people.

Get out into your community and get to know your neighbors. Too many Christians live in a glass house where they only spend time with church people. Get out in the community and be an authentic Christian day after day. To be a living witness does not remove a Christian's responsibility to share the faith; rather it gives the opportunity. Jesus said in Matthew 5:16 to let your light shine before men. A Christian's life becomes a light for others to see God. Therefore, believers should show the world that our God is real through actions and deeds. In the words of St. Francis, "Preach at all times, but if you must, use words."

When you get into the community, you will begin to see what the needs of the people are. This is how your family will begin to develop a heart for your community. We began to canvas our city and assess the needs of the people. When we began to look around our city we saw many people with tremendous needs. Make a personal inventory of the needs, and then you will be able to minister to the needs of your community.

If you are going to be a missional family, you must also effectively communicate the needs of your community to your children. Let them know the facts about the needs in your community and the world. Tell others how they can help. I have learned that children want to help if they are properly informed. Communication is the key. You will be amazed how willing your kids will be to join the cause of reaching your city and the world.

Being a missional family is also working with others to make a difference in our communities for Christ. Do not try to do it all alone or try to reinvent the wheel. Partner with others that are already doing ministry in your church or community. The needs are great, but if we begin to work with others, we can make a difference in our cities and communities. Working with others is a powerful witness of Christ's love and shows people how Christians are essential to the community.

My local church has taught me the powerful meaning of being a missional family. As a church, we have always looked for ways to involve our families in mission. We have adopted beach accesses, which the church cleaned once a month to show the community that the church cares about the beaches. The church began an art-mentoring program that reached at-risk youth in our community. The church hosted art shows for young people that have reached hundreds of young people from the community. We even opened an art gallery that hosted art shows and concerts to build bridges between the church and community. Recently, our families have been involved with sending cows to Africa, Christmas shoe boxes around the world through Samaritan's Purse, and sponsoring children through World Vision.

Grow at Home

Maybe you're ready and thinking to yourself, "I'm in! So now what?" Here are some practical thoughts and ideas that will help you explore being missional as a family together. This is certainly not an exhaustive list, but it will give a starting place to become a launching pad for mission in and through your family.

1. Prayer is a powerful teaching tool to help give children a burden for the lost and hurting. Pray for the people in your community, for missionaries, for global poverty, etc.
2. Get out and learn the needs in your community. Be informed about the needs of missionaries and Christians around the world, especially those suffering in persecution and poverty.
3. Get a map or globe of the world and share with your children about unreached people groups. Let them know about global poverty and the rise of persecution of Christians around the world.
4. One of the best ways to teach your children about mission is to sponsor a child through World Vision or Compassion International.

5. At Christmas time, have your children fill shoe boxes through Samaritan's Purse. Let your kids pick out everything that goes in the shoebox. Pray over it as you pack and send it off.

6. Begin to save your change or do a yard sale to raise money for missions. This can be an easy way to teach kids about missions.

7. Reading missionary biographies to your children is a wonderful way to give them a heart for missions.

8. Find ways locally to serve others. Take your children with you to soup kitchens or food banks, or to pick up trash at your local park.

9. Invite unchurched people to dinner, for a play date, or to a church group.

10. Make your children aware of the needs of orphans around the world, even right in your own city. A wonderful book on orphan care is *Orphanology: Awakening to Gospel-Centered Adoption and Orphan Care* by Tony Merida and Rick Morton.

Chapter 8

Following Jesus through the Church Year

"The church calendar aims at nothing less than to change the way we experience time and perceive reality."

—*Mark Galli*

Every year, my family and I look forward to the different seasons. As I write this, my family is getting ready for Christmas. We have begun to develop our own family traditions, like getting our Christmas tree, baking cookies, and reading the Christmas story together. Each season brings its own

unique rhythm, weather, traditions, and memories.
Spring, summer, fall, and winter can be powerful
reminders of the seasons and rhythms of the spiritual
life. The Christian life has different seasons, just as
nature has seasons. Each of these seasons remind us
of the multidimensional nature of discipleship.

The early church began to remember the various
themes of the gospel of Jesus Christ by celebrating
different seasons of the Christian year. By the fourth
century, churches in the Holy Land began to develop
liturgies to mark the days of Holy Week and Easter
at holy sites to commemorate the life and death of
Jesus. Pilgrims began to travel to Jerusalem to partici-
pate in these ceremonies and eventually brought the
practices back with them to their countries of origin.
Today, many different Christian traditions continue
to place an important role on remembering the
seasons of the Christian year.

The Seasons of the Church Year

The church year involves an annual cycle of seasons
including Advent, Epiphany, Lent, Easter, Pentecost,
and Ordinary. Each season has its own unique set
of prayers and themes that center on the gospel of
Jesus Christ and prepare us for our journey of faith.

Here is a quick overview of the seasons of the church calendar and their meanings that will help your family celebrate each season in the home.

The season of Advent marks the beginning of the church year for Christians all over the world. It begins on the fourth Sunday before Christmas Day, which is the Sunday nearest November 30, and ends on Christmas Eve (December 24). During Advent, we prepare our hearts for the mystery of the incarnation by focusing on the virgin birth and the faith of the Virgin Mary, the shepherds, and the wise men.

The season following Christmas is Epiphany, in which the church proclaims Jesus to the world as Son of God, Lord, and King. In many churches, it remembers the coming of the wise men bringing gifts to the Christ child, whereby they reveal Jesus to the world as Lord and King. This season places a strong emphasis on the human nature of Christ. Epiphany means "manifestation," "appearance," or "vision of God."

At Lent, we remember Christ's temptation, suffering, and death. During Easter, we celebrate the glorious resurrection of Christ. Lent is a forty-day period beginning on Ash Wednesday that concludes

the day before Easter. The climax of Lent is Holy
Week, which is the week immediately preceding
Easter or Resurrection Sunday. It is observed in
many Christian churches as a time to commemorate
and reenact the last week of Jesus' life, His suffering
(passion), and His death, through various obser-
vances and services of worship.

The Easter season is the fifty days from
Resurrection Sunday to Pentecost Sunday. Easter
season celebrates the fact that "Christ is Risen!" It
recognizes God's ongoing work of establishing a new
creation through the resurrection of Jesus Christ. It
also celebrates the hope of that work being culmi-
nated in a new heaven and a new earth.

Literally meaning "fifty days after," the day of
Pentecost falls fifty days after Easter. At Pentecost,
we celebrate the coming of the Holy Spirit into our
lives and the church. The season is used to celebrate
the reality that God, through the power of His Holy
Spirit, continues to work in, through, and among
His people.

The final season is commonly referred to as
Ordinary Time. The season's name comes, not from
ordinary, but the word "ordinal," which means
counted time. The time, beginning on the first Sunday

after Pentecost, is used to focus on specific themes of interest or importance to a local church.

Grow at Home

The seasons of the Christian year have been a wonderful discipleship tool that the church has used to celebrate the major events of the life of Jesus and the kingdom of God for centuries. The seasons of the church year can also be a helpful way for your family to celebrate the major themes of the gospel of Jesus Christ in the home with your children. Throughout the year, you can follow the seasons with your children with meaningful traditions that include Bible readings, prayers, and crafts.

Here are some fun ideas that will help you celebrate the two biggest seasons of the Christian year, Advent and Lent, with your family.

The Adventure of Advent

Advent is my favorite season of the Christian year. I love the colors, sights, and smells of the season. Advent reminds us of the mystery of the virgin birth of our Savior Jesus Christ. Here are a few ideas to help you celebrate the season together.

1. Make an Advent wreath with your children. Making an Advent wreath can be fun and easy. Each week there is a different candle, scripture, and prayer.
2. Make a Jesse tree, which is a depiction in art of the ancestors of Christ.
3. Set up or create a nativity set with your children. One of the simplest ways to remember the Christmas story with your children is to enact the Christmas story by setting out a nativity set.
4. Visit a nursing home and sing carols to residents.
5. Take some time to make homemade decorations and decorate the Christmas tree together.
6. Shop and give gifts to a child or a family in need.
7. Go caroling in your neighborhood with your family or other church members.
8. Take a night and talk about what Advent means to you.
9. Read the Christmas story together from the Bible.
10. Give a gift and change a life by sponsoring a child or giving an animal or a micro loan through an organization like Compassion International or World Vision.

Bringing Lent to Life

Lent is a wonderful season as we remember the last days of Jesus, His death, burial, and resurrection. Here are ten ideas to help you bring Lent to life as you celebrate this season with your family.

1. During Lent you can give up things like fast food, TV, technology, sweets, electronic games, using the computer, or buying anything that is unneeded.

2. As a reminder that we are like clay in God's hands, shatter inexpensive clay pots and give each family member a piece to keep during Lent.

3. During Lent, plan simple meals and let everyone at your table share an idea for helping hungry people. Save the extra money to give to others in need. Ask God to help you carry out one of these ideas.

4. Slow down and plan time together and enrich your family life. This time for families at home can include prayer, devotions, crafts, art, games, and meals.

5. Pretzels have their origin in the early church, and they were traditionally made of only flour, salt, and water. Pretzels were shaped in the form of

arms crossed in prayer. Choose one night in Lent to make pretzels. Find a recipe on the Internet.

6. Go through your house and give away unused toys and clothes to the poor. Or have a yard sale and donate the profits to your favorite charity.

7. Choose something good you can do each day of Lent like helping a neighbor, visiting a nursing home, or making cookies or a meal for a shut in.

8. Eggs remind us of the new life that is in the resurrection of Jesus Christ. When you dye Easter eggs, think about what the colors mean: red—Jesus' blood, purple—royalty, green— new life, gold—resurrection.

9. Plant a seed to teach your children about the resurrection and rebirth. Explain how planting a seed symbolizes the death of Jesus and how the sprouting seed symbolizes His rebirth.

10. Have your children make artwork like a colorful cross, or posters that say "He Is Risen!" or "Our Redeemer Lives!" and hang them on the wall, door, or refrigerator.

Chapter 9

Introducing Your Children to Jesus

"Every child, therefore, you are to watch over with the utmost care, that, when you are called to give an account of each to the Father of Spirits, you may give your accounts with joy and not with grief."

—John Wesley

no book on family discipleship would be complete without talking about the importance of introducing your children to Jesus Christ. What good is it if we raise good kids, with good morals, and a proper upbringing, but who do not have a personal relationship with Jesus Christ? These things are all good, however, our ultimate goal in Christian parenting is to introduce our children to Jesus Christ. The purpose of this chapter is to give you a brief overview of the life of Jesus to help you share Christ with your children.

Children are never too young to come to faith in Christ. Jesus reminds us of his love for children: "Let the little children come to me and do not hinder them, for to such belongs the kingdom of heaven" (Matt. 19:14). Statistics show that children are open to the gospel and ready to receive Jesus Christ as Lord and Savior. In fact, most Christians come to faith before becoming an adult. A current Barna study indicates that nearly half of all Americans who accept Jesus Christ as their Savior do so before reaching the age of thirteen (43 percent), and that two out of three born-again Christians (64 percent) made that commitment to Christ before their eighteenth birthday.[1]

Who Was Jesus?

Never before has there been such a need to understand who Jesus was and is. Even in the first century, there were various opinions and points of view as to who Jesus was. And today, people are more confused than ever about Jesus. There are even diverse points of view and widespread confusion about Jesus in the church today. Being a Christian begins and ends with Jesus Christ. After all, doesn't being a Christian mean that you believe in Jesus? The word *Christian* literally means "Christ-like." Therefore, a proper understanding of the life of Jesus Christ is the place to start if we are going to introduce our children to Christ.

Let's begin with the simple question, "Who was Jesus?" There was an actual man named Jesus who said and did things that were considered to be remarkable. Historically speaking, he was a Jewish teacher, prophet, and miracle worker. His followers believed that He was the Jewish Messiah or the Son of God. As a result, His followers began to collect information about what He said and did.

It is widely accepted that Jesus was an actual person who walked the earth. But what do we know about His origins? According to the gospel of Luke, the angel Gabriel was sent from God to the Virgin Mary. He told her that the Holy Ghost would come upon her and she would conceive a child in her womb, who would be the Son of God, and that He should be named Jesus. The virgin birth was miraculous because Mary became pregnant without having a sexual relationship. God supernaturally placed the seed in her womb.

Jesus was born in Bethlehem of Judea near Jerusalem. The birth of Jesus is the most important event in the history of the world. On the night Jesus was born, the Bible says that angels visited shepherds on the Judean hillside while they were watching their sheep. The angels announced that Jesus, the promised Messiah, had been born. The shepherds immediately went to see the newborn Jesus. Jesus was born in a humble manger in a barn among the animals. Wise men came from distant lands after they saw the bright star in the sky signifying that the promised Savior had been born. They brought gifts and worshiped the tiny baby boy.

The virgin birth of Jesus Christ is one of the central doctrines of the Christian faith, commonly referred to as the incarnation. *Incarnation* means "to become flesh." The incarnation reveals Jesus' divinity and humanity. The Bible affirms that Jesus was fully both God and man. Jesus was born of a woman, experienced childhood, had a family, got hungry and thirsty, and worked as a carpenter. He experienced happiness, sadness, temptation, and compassion. As the Son of God, He forgave sins, healed the sick, was sinless, received worship, and said that He was the only way to heaven.

The four Gospels also record important information about the life and ministry of Jesus Christ. Jesus ministered for only three years, beginning at the age of thirty. He began to teach and to perform many miracles in all the communities near His hometown of Galilee. Jesus often used parables to explain spiritual truths when teaching the multitudes that followed Him. Some of these teachings and miracles are recorded in the Bible. Multitudes of people followed Jesus—hearing His teachings and witnessing His miracles.

Jesus declared that His purpose in life was to do the will of His heavenly Father. Wherever He went, He did good and healed those who were oppressed by the devil (see Acts 10:38). He never hurt or injured anyone, although He was at times angry with the self-righteous church-going people. Just because they were religious did not mean that they knew God. Jesus was a friend to sinners and the outcasts of society. He reached out to everyone, including the publicans, thieves, and prostitutes.

The Death of Jesus

The religious leaders did not like Jesus so they devised a plan to kill Him. He was only thirty-three years of age. They made false statements about Him in court and demanded that Pontius Pilate sentence Jesus to die.

Jesus was thrown into a prison and Roman soldiers beat Him with a whip. His flesh was torn and blood ran down His back. Jesus was forced to carry His own cross down the back streets of Jerusalem and up the hill to Golgotha. He was nailed to a cross of rough wood that was thrust into the ground, and He hung on the cross where people mocked and scorned Him for calling Himself the Son of God.

As He died, Jesus asked, "Father, forgive them, for they do not know what they do." He pronounced, "It is finished!" as He died. He was an obedient Son. The instant He died, the heavy veil of the temple was torn in half from the top down. The sky was dark as night.

The Bible tells us that He is the only Savior of the world, having shed His own blood and dying a vicarious death on Calvary's cross. By His death, He took our place, He revealed the divine love and upheld divine justice, removing our guilt and reconciling us to God.

The Resurrection

Friends of Jesus took His body down from the cross and buried Him in a borrowed tomb. The Romans assigned soldiers to guard Jesus' grave because the Jews were afraid that Jesus' body would be stolen. To prevent this from happening, a very heavy stone was rolled across the tomb and it was sealed shut.

After Jesus died on the cross, He rose bodily from the grave on the third day. When some of Jesus' followers came to the tomb and found it empty, they were afraid. Jesus then appeared to His followers outside the tomb. He appeared for a period of forty days to more than five hundred witnesses, performing many convincing proofs of His resurrection. The apostle Paul summed up the life, death, and resurrection of Jesus by saying "that Christ died for our sins in accordance with the Scriptures, that he was buried, that he was raised on the third day in accordance with the Scriptures, and that he appeared to Cephas, then to the twelve" (1 Cor. 15:3–5).

The resurrection is one of the hallmarks of the Christian faith. The Bible says, "If Christ has not been raised, then our preaching is in vain and your faith is in vain" (1 Cor. 15:14). Because Jesus was resurrected from the dead, you and I have the promise that we will also come back to life and live with Jesus, if we believe in Him as our Lord and Savior.

After His resurrection, Jesus ascended into heaven where, at God's right hand, He intercedes for His people and rules as Lord over all. He is the head of His body, the church, and should be adored, loved, served, and obeyed by all. As He was leaving, Jesus promised to return again.

Grow at Home

So how do children become Christians? It is no different for children than it is for adults. It's simple, yet deeply profound. Becoming a Christian begins with God's free offer of salvation through His Son Jesus Christ. Jesus began His ministry with the declaration, "The time is fulfilled, and the kingdom of God is at hand; repent and believe in the gospel" (Mark 1:15). According to the Bible, we must repent and believe in Jesus as Lord. The word *repent* simply means to "turn" or "change one's mind." The first step is to repent and turn away from our sins to turn to God in faith. This is the starting place for receiving the gospel.

The next step is to believe the good news, which is the meaning of the word *gospel*. The word *believe* literally means "a firm persuasion, or trust" in God. Belief is at the heart of what it means to be a Christian. The Bible clearly tells us that we must believe that Jesus is Lord. Paul puts it into clear perspective by telling us, "If you confess with your mouth that Jesus is Lord and believe in your heart that God raised him from the dead, you will be saved" (Rom. 10:9). All we need to do is put our faith and hope in Jesus as Lord and Savior. Encourage your child to simply trust in Him alone to save them through what He has done for them on the cross. Ask them to surrender their life to Him today and begin to follow Him.

Jesus asked His disciples, "Who do you say that I am?" (Mark 8:29). Likewise, we must ask ourselves the same question and decide for ourselves. In the end, a person must either accept the claims of the Bible in faith or dismiss them entirely. C. S. Lewis wrote,

> A man who was merely a man and said the sort of things Jesus said would not be a great moral teacher. He would either be a lunatic—on the level with a man who says he is a poached egg— or he would be the devil of hell. You must make your choice. Either this man was, and is, the Son of God; or else a madman or something worse. You can shut Him up for a fool; you can spit at Him and kill Him for a demon; or you can fall at His feet and call Him Lord and God. But

let us not come with any patronizing nonsense about His being a great human teacher. He has not left that open to us. He did not intend to.[2]

As we end this chapter, it is important to remember that while we play a vital a role in bringing our children to faith, it is ultimately God who saves our children. We can teach our children about Christ, but salvation is ultimately God's work. Knowing this will keep us from spiritual pride and thinking that we somehow caused our children's salvation. Our role as parents is to live and to share the gospel, while it is always God that saves. Therefore, as parents, we do our part and then watch God's Spirit work in our children's hearts.

Ideas for Leading Your Child to Christ

As you prepare to discuss salvation with your child, here are a few things to keep in mind.

1. Rest in God's timing. Salvation belongs to God, so rest in the fact that He is at work in the life of your child.
2. Spend time in prayer. Ask the Holy Spirit to prepare your child's heart to receive the gospel message in faith.

3. Read the Bible regularly. The Word says, "Faith comes from hearing, and hearing *through the word of Christ*" (Rom. 10:17, italics mine). Our children need to hear the Word of God to open their hearts and minds to their need of salvation.

4. Teach your Children the gospel. Talk to your children about what God has done for them through the life, death, and resurrection of Jesus Christ.

5. Talk to them in a conversational way. Use simple words your child will understand and try to avoid theological terminology and phrases that might confuse your child.

6. Don't force or coerce your child to make a decision. Your child's salvation is a matter between God and your child. The Holy Spirit must be the one who convicts your child of their sin and need for salvation.

Notes

Chapter 1: A Parent's Responsibility

1. See Michael Nazir-Ali, *Triple Jeopardy for the West: Aggressive Secularism, Radical Islamism and Multiculturalism* (London, UK: Bloomsbury Publishing, 2012).
2. Alan Hirsch, *The Forgotten Ways: Reactivating the Missional Church* (Grand Rapids, MI: Brazos Press, 2006), 45.

Chapter 2: Rediscovering Family Worship

1. Jason Helopoulos, *A Neglected Grace: Family Worship in the Christian Home* (Scotland, UK: Christian Focus Publications, 2013), 13–14.
2. Jonathan Edwards, "Farewell Sermon," *The Works of Jonathan Edwards*, vol. I, p. ccvi; http://www.ccel.org /ccel/edwards/works1.html.

Chapter 4: Teaching Children Truths through Catechism

1. Richard Baxter, *The Reformed Pastor*, (Carlisle, PA: The Banner of Truth, 1974), 177.

2. See my book *Creed: Connect to the Basic Essentials of Historic Christian Faith* (Colorado Springs, CO: NavPress, 2011).
3. The word "catholic" here means universal.

Chapter 5: Cultivating Character through the Fruits of the Spirit

1. John Yates and Susan Alexander Yates, *Raising Kids with Character That Lasts* (Grand Rapids, MI: Revell, 1992), 13.

Chapter 6: Learning to Pray the Lord's Prayer

1. Parts of this chapter first appeared in my book *Creed: Connect to the Basic Essentials of Historic Christian Faith* (Colorado Springs, CO: NavPress, 2011).

Chapter 7: Becoming a Missional Family

1. Ed Stetzer, *Planting Missional Churches: Planting a Church That's Biblically Sound and Reaching People in Culture* (Nashville, TN: B&H Academic, 2006), 19.
2. George G. Hunter, *Celtic Way of Evangelism* (Nashville, TN: Abingdon Press, 2000), 53.

Chapter 9: Introducing Your Children to Jesus

1. "Evangelism Is Most Effective Among Kids." October 11, 2004. https://www.barna.org/barna-update/article/5-barna-update/196-evangelism-is-most-effective-among-kids#.U4O-riinBSo.
2. C. S. Lewis, *Mere Christianity* (London: Harper Collins, 1952), 54–56.